KANJI de MANGA

Vol. 4

MANGA UNIVERSITY presents...

The Comic Book That Teaches You How To Read And Write Japanese!

Japanime

TOKYO SAN FRANCISCO

Manga University Presents ... Kanji de Manga
The Comic Book That Teaches You
How To Read And Write Japanese
Volume Four

Published by Manga University under the auspices of Japanime Co. Ltd.,
3-31-18 Nishi-Kawaguchi, Kawaguchi-shi, Saitama-ken 332–0021, Japan.

www.mangauniversity.com

ISBN-13: 978-4-921205-09-6
ISBN-10: 4-921205-09-4

07 08 09 10　10 9 8 7 6 5 4 3 2

Printed in Canada

CONTENTS

The Manga University Mission Statement

The mission of Manga University is to enlighten and educate the international community on all aspects of Japanese culture through the creative use of traditional manga artwork.

The university recognizes that manga transcends mainstream entertainment and possesses a unique ability to convey the true spirit of Japan, making the art form an ideal communicative tool to touch the lives and inspire the minds of Japan enthusiasts worldwide.

Our mission and philosophy are firmly rooted in the principles and conviction of the Japanese educational tradition and in the best ideals of Japanese heritage.

Founded at the turn of the century and located in Tokyo, Manga University is one of the world's foremost publishers of manga-themed educational materials.

INTRODUCTION

This may be an odd way to begin a language book, but I'd like to share with you a little inside information about the publishing industry.

It has to do, of course, with language books and in particular language series, such as this one. We were once upon a time given some advice: Whatever you do, don't publish a language book – and especially don't publish a series of language books.

The reasoning behind this is that people who decide to learn a language often don't stick with it. And, as a result, each volume in a series about language will sell less than the previous volume.

If you followed that logic, eventually you'd end up with a book that no one will purchase. And that, for a publisher of books, would be very bad business indeed. But we at Manga University

know something they don't—something about you, and something about our books. We know that you are not just someone studying a language, but a true student of Japanese culture. For you, this is more than just a phase or a hobby, it is a passion fueled by a desire.

And we know that our books, filled with great manga characters teaching kanji, are quite simply the easiest and friendliest way you can learn Japanese writing, completely unlike anything else out there. Manga University strives to take one of the world's most daunting syllabaries and place it within your grasp. All you need now is just a little more hard work—something you've been doing all along, and very well, or else you wouldn't be holding this book in your hands.

And now that you are holding this book, you know just how wrong our business advisers were.

As with any learning institution, Manga University's singular goal is the spread of knowledge. And as with any university, our success or failure is entirely dependant on the strength of our students. You have proven yourself to be a true student of language and culture, and thankfully, as you enter this new and most challenging phase yet, you have some help. All your manga friends are back, and no matter how difficult it gets, they simply won't let you give up.

Just as you've committed to learning this language, we're committed to helping you.

Now let's not waste any more time—it's time to turn this page, and continue your fine Manga University education.

Gambare!

PAGE GUIDE

① The featured kanji

② Common definition

③ Readings: kun-yomi (Japanese readings) are written in hiragana, while on-yomi (Chinese readings) are in katakana.

④ Examples of compounds containing the featured kanji, their pronunciations (written in hiragana) and English definitions. (An asterisk next to a compound indicates that one or more of its kanji are not featured in this or any of the previous volumes of the "Kanji de Manga" series.)

⑤ Stroke order: In general, the strokes are written from top to bottom and left to right. For a list of additional stroke-order rules, please refer to the chart at the back of this book.

⑥ The manga. All dialogue is written in hiragana and katakana except for the single featured kanji. The proper pronunciation of the kanji is indicated in furigana (tiny hiragana) written above the character.

⑦ Translation of the dialogue and selected onomatopoeia.

STUDY SECTION

MATCH / FIT

あ(う)、あ(わす)、カッ、ガッ、ゴウ

ex. 合う (あう) - to match

ex. 合唱* (がっしょう) - chorus

ex. 合計 (ごうけい) - total

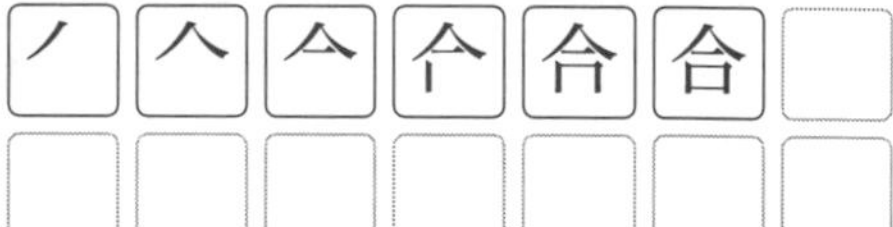

うぅぅぅううう!
むきーーっ
だ…
だいじょうぶ!?

パズルのピースが、なかなか
合わなくて…。ついつい……。
できあがりが
たのしみね。
がんばって。

Boy: うううううう！
Arrrrrggg!

むきーっ (screech)

Girl: だ、だいじょうぶ！？
Are you all right!?

Boy: パズルのピースが、なかなか
合わなくて… ついつい…
This puzzle piece doesn't match... I just...

Girl: できあがりがたのしみね。
がんばって。I can tell you really want to finish it. Keep trying!

HEAD

あたま、ズ、トウ

ex. 先頭 (せんとう) - head
ex. 頭痛* (ずつう) - headache
ex. 石頭 (いしあたま) - inflexible person

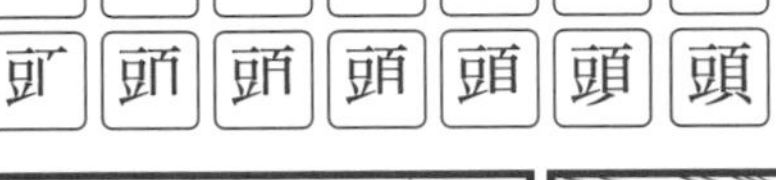

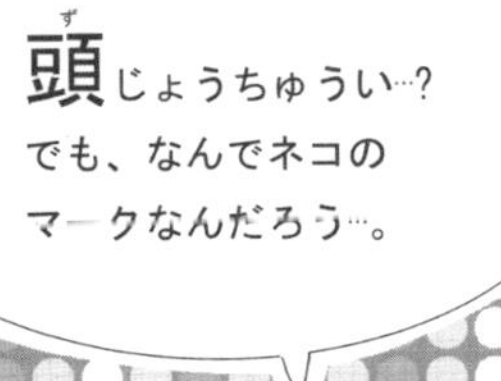

たしっ
ズリ…
頭(あたま)のうえに
ネコが
とびのって
くるからか…。

Boy: 頭じょうちゅうい？
でも、なんでネコの
マークなんだろう。
Watch your head?
But why the cat?

Sign: 頭上ちゅうい (Watch Your Head)

たしっ (crash landing)

ズリ… (droop)

Boy: 頭のうえにネコが
とびのってくるからか…
Because of cats falling
onto your head...

HIT

あ(たる)、あ(てる)、トウ

ex. 当たる (あたる) - to be hit
ex. 当番 (とうばん) - on duty
ex. 当選* (とうせん) - winning the prize

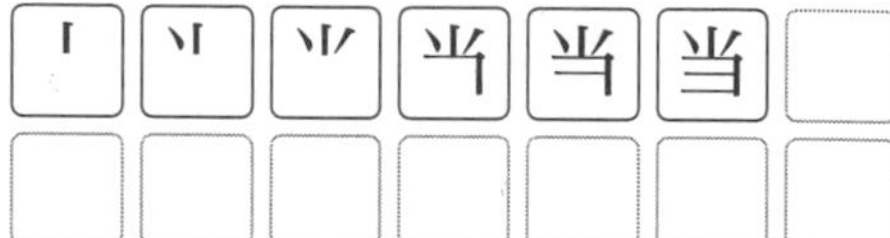

Clerk: 1とうしょうおお当たり〜！
You won first prize!

カラン カラン (ring ring)

コロン… (plink)

Sign: ふくびきたいかい
(Raffle)

Woman: わああああっ
Yaaay!

BREATH

いき、ソク

ex. ため息 (ためいき) - sigh
ex. 休息 (きゅうそく) - rest
ex. 喘息* (ぜんそく) - asthma

Son: とうさん
もう息きれてる
じゃないか
だらしないなぁ！
Dad, you're out of breath already!
What a sissy!

ぜーはー (panting)

Father: う、うんどうで…
息こに…ま…まけ…
まけるなんて…
My son...beats me...at jogging...
How embarrassing...

POND

いけ、チ

ex. 池 (いけ) - pond
ex. 溜池* (ためいけ) - reservoir
ex. 人口池* (じんこういけ) - man-made lake

Babysitter: 池におちないように、じゅうぶんきをつけなさいよー！
I want you to be really careful not to fall into the pond!

Boy: わかってる！
I know!

がくんっ (stumbling)

ドッポーン (splash)

Babysitter: だから… 池におちないようにっていったのに…。
I warned you...not to fall into the pond...

STONE

いし、シャク、セキ

ex. 磁石* (じしゃく) - magnet
ex. 宝石* (ほうせき) - jewel
ex. 石油* (せきゆ) - oil; petroleum

Girl: あら？
Huh?

キラッ (twinkle)

わぁあっ。なんてきれいな石！
Wow. What a pretty stone!

ほう石みたいだわ。
It looks like a jewel.

CITY / MARKET

いち、シ

ex. 市場 (しじょう) - market
ex. 市民* (しみん) - citizen
ex. 都市 (とし) - urban city

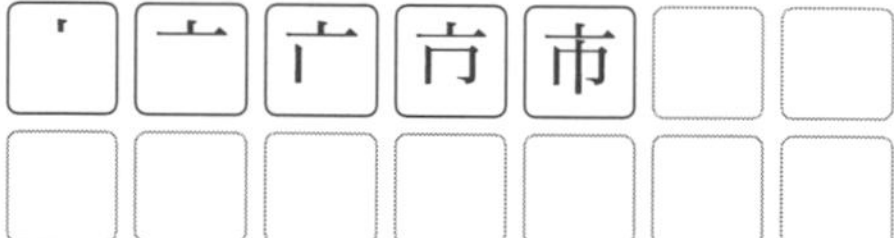

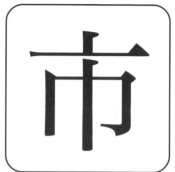

First boy: さすがはうお市ばだねー。
It's the fish market!

きょろきょろ (curiously looking around)

First boy: さかなもひともたくさんいるよ。
There sure are lots of fish and people.

Second boy: きんじょのひとも かいにこられる市ばなんだよ。
Even the local residents like to come to this market.

THREAD

いと、シ

ex. 糸くず (いとくず) - thread
ex. 毛糸 (けいと) - knitting wool
ex. 製糸* (せいし) - filature

ん……?
糸くずがついてる。

糸くずとってあげよっ。
すっ

Girl: ん…?
Huh…?
糸くずがついてる。
There's a loose thread on her dress.

Girl: 糸くずとってあげよう。
Why don't I just pick it off.
すっ (quietly reaching out)
Girl: わぁぁぁぁ! Woooaaahhh!
しゅるしゅる (sound of thread coming undone)
オロオロ (sound of panic)

ROCK

いわ、ガン

ex. 岩場 (いわば) - rocky area
ex. 岩登り* (いわのぼり) - rock climbing
ex. 岩石 (がんせき) - rock

First boy scout: あの岩…
うごいてない?
Isn't that rock… shaking?

ぐらぐら (rocking noise)

Second boy scout: えっ!?
What!?

ゴロゴロゴロ (sound of rolling rock)

Both boy scouts: ギャアアアアア
Aaahhh!

INSIDE

うち、ナイ

ex. 身内 (みうち) - relatives
ex. 案内* (あんない) - guidance
ex. 内緒* (ないしょ) - secret

……。
ザワ
ザワ
ザワ
ザワ
ザワ
あしもとの せんより内がわに はいっていて くださいね。

つぎは、しせつの内ぶを あん内しますねー。
わーい
ザワ
ザワ
ザワ
わかりました一！

Tour guide: つぎは、しせつの内ぶを
あん内しますねー。
Next, I'll show you the inside of the building.

People in crowd: わーい
わかりましたー！
Yay! We understand!

ザワザワ (chatter)

Visitor: (speechless)

Tour guide: あしもとの
せんより内がわにはいってい
てくださいね。
Please stay inside the line on the floor.

HORSE

うま、バ

ex. 馬 (うま) - horse
ex. 馬車 (ばしゃ) - coach
ex. 競馬* (けいば) - horse racing

丨	𠃌	冂	冃	冄	馬	馬
馬	馬	馬				

そのうち、はく馬にのった おうじさまが…わたしをさがしに あらわれるはずよ～！
……。

まちなかで 馬にのるなんて あぶないよ…。
ムキーッ
うーん…

Girl: そのうち、はく馬にのった おうじさまが… わたしをさがしに あらわれるはずよ～！
Someday my prince will come, riding on a white horse, and searching for me!

Boy: まちなかで馬にのるなんて あぶないよ…。
I think it would be dangerous to ride a horse in the city...

うーん (Hmmm...)
ムキーッ (frustrated)

PICTURE

エ、カイ

ex. 絵葉書* (えはがき) - picture postcard

ex. 絵の具* (えのぐ) - colors

ex. 絵画 (かいが) - picture

なにを
かいているの?
絵てがみよ。

ことばだけより、絵もつけたほうがきもちもつたわりそうで。
すごーい。
きっと、もらったひともよろこぶよ。

First girl: なにをかいているの？
What are you writing?

Second girl: 絵てがみよ。
It's a letter with drawings.

Second girl: ことばだけより、絵もつけたほうがきもちもつたわりそうで。
I guess illustrations help me express my feelings more than words.

First girl: すごーい。きっと、もらったひともよろこぶよ。Wow! I'm sure whomever you send it to will love it.

GARDEN

エン

ex. 公園 (こうえん) - park
ex. 遊園地* (ゆうえんち) - amusement park
ex. 庭園* (ていえん) - garden

First girl: わぁ！このゆう園ちって どうぶつ園もあるんだ。
Wow! This amusement park also has its own zoo.

Sign: どうぶつ園 (Zoo)

Second girl: あとでどうぶつ園も いってみようよ！
We should definitely check the zoo out later!

KING

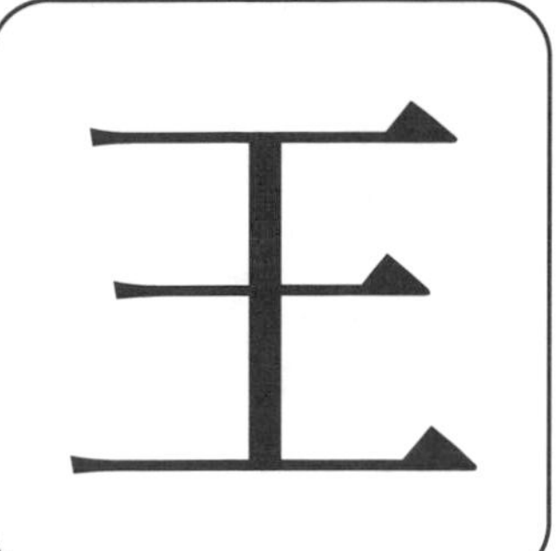

オウ

ex. 王様* (おうさま) - king
ex. 王子 (おうじ) - prince
ex. 大王 (だいおう) - great king

Boy: やったぞー。
I did it!

王さまきぶんをあじわうために
王かんをつくってみたぞー！
This crown I made will make me feel just like a king!

ズルッ (slipping down)

おおきすぎちゃった
みたい…。
Looks like it's too big...

SUBJECT

カ

ex. 科学 (かがく) - science
ex. 教科書 (きょうかしょ) - textbook
ex. 百科事典* (ひゃっかじてん) - encyclopedia

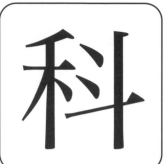

一	二	千	禾	禾	禾	禾
科	科					

Schoolgirl: もう、こんなじかん！あしたのきょう科のよういをしなくちゃ。
Wow, look at the time! I've got to prepare for my classes tomorrow.

えーと…。
科もくは、科がくと…
こくごと…。
Let's see…
The subjects I have tomorrow are science... Japanese, and...

SHELL

かい

ex. 貝 (かい) - shell
ex. ほら貝 (ほらがい) - conch
ex. 烏貝 (からすがい) - fresh-water mussel

Girl: 貝がらにみみをあてるとなみのおとがするのよ。
If you hold a shell up to your ear you can hear the ocean.

うっとり…
(enchanted)

Boy: へぇ～。そうなんだ。
Really? Is that so?

Boy: なんにもきこえないよー。
I don't hear a thing.

Girl: まったくムードがないわね！
You are so unromantic!

FACE

かお、ガン

ex. 顔見知り (かおみしり) - acquaintance
ex. 笑顔* (えがお) - smile
ex. 顔面* (がんめん) - face

Boy: くすくす。
(snickering)

キュッキュ (squeak squeak)

ぐうぐう (snoring)

Father: うわぁぁぁ!
へんな顔になってるぅぅぅ!
Whaaaa! My face is all weird!

ガーン (sound of shock)

NUMBER

かず、かぞ(える)、スウ

ex. 数 (かず) - number
ex. 数える (かぞえる) - to count
ex. 数学 (すうがく) - mathematics

Office worker: 数えることはすきなんだけど…。
I don't mind counting, but...

どーん (sound representing abundance)

にん数がたりないと、数えるのもひとくろう…。
Counting these all by myself is a bit tough...

アンケートの数がおおいとたいへんなのよね…。 It sure is a lot of work when there are so many surveys...

FORM / SHAPE

かた、かたち、ギョウ、ケイ

ex. 形 (かたち) - shape
ex. 人形 (にんぎょう) - doll
ex. 形式* (けいしき) - form; formality

Girl: このへんな形のものはなに?
What is this weird-shaped thing?

Boy: ケ…ケーキつくったつもり…。
W...well I planned to bake a cake...

ぎょっ (scared)

プスプス (sound of steam)

Boy: 形はともかく。
あじはいいとおもうんだよね。
Don't pay attention to the shape. I think it should taste just fine.

Girl: (speechless)

BLADE / SWORD

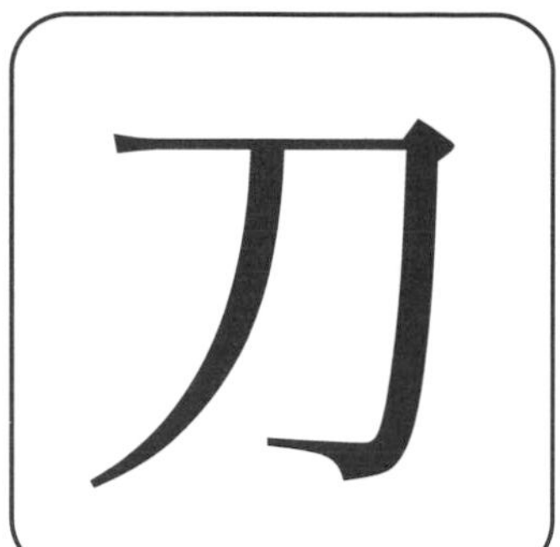

かたな、トウ

ex. 刀 (かたな) - blade
ex. 日本刀 (にほんとう) - Japanese sword
ex. 木刀 (ぼくとう) - wooden sword

すちゃっ (clank)

Sister: そっ…
その刀ってほんもの！？
What the… Is that sword real!?

Brother : にせものだよ。でも、刀をもつと
さむらいきぶんだよ。It's fake, but carrying a sword makes me feel like a samurai.

Sister: あぶなそうだから刀はふりまわさ
ないでね。Don't swing that sword around, OK? It looks dangerous.

ENERGY

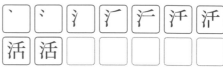

カツ

ex. 新生活* (しんせいかつ) - new life
ex. 活動 (かつどう) - activity
ex. 活気 (かっき) - energy; liveliness

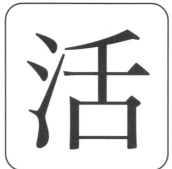

ひっこしも
かんりょう！
ガラ
しんせい活がんばるぞー！
活きにみちたものに
するぞー！

あ……。

New neighbor: ひっこしもかんりょう！
I'm done moving!

ガラ (sound of window sliding open)
しんせい活がんばるぞー！
活きにみちたものにするぞー！
I'm gonna live my new life to the fullest!

あ…
Oh…

かぁぁ (blushing)

くすくす (giggling)

CORNER / HORN

かど、つの、カク

ex. 街角* (まちかど) - street corner

ex. 角笛* (つのぶえ) - horn

ex. 三角 (さんかく) - triangle

いたぁぁぁぁぁぁぁぁぁぁあっっ！
じたばた
じたばた
なにが
あったの!?

Boy: いたぁぁあっ！
Ouuuch!

じたばた (struggling around)

Girl: なにがあったの！？
What happened!?

Boy: あしのこゆびを角にぶつけちゃった…！
I stubbed my pinkie toe on the corner.

ぷくぅ～ (swelling up)

Girl: (speechless)

門

GATE

かど、モン

ex. 門松 (かどまつ) - New Year's decoration

ex. 正門 (せいもん) - main gate

ex. 校門 (こうもん) - school gate

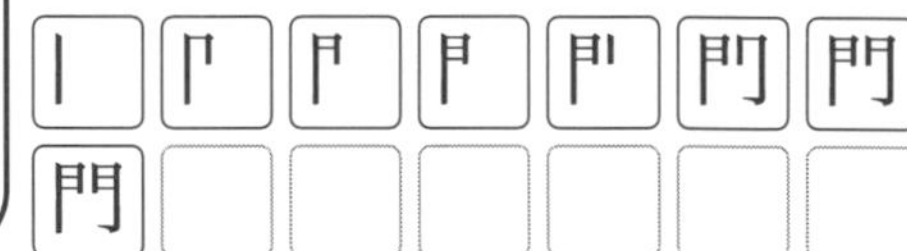

American girl: これはなにかしら？
I wonder what this is...

Japanese boy: 門まつって
いうものだよ。
That's called a "kadomatsu."

Japanese boy: しんねんに
門のところにかざるんだよ。
You place them at gates as decorations during New Year's.

American girl: ほんとうだー。
Oh, really.

YELLOW

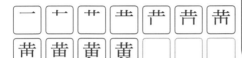

き、オウ

ex. 黄色 (きいろ) - yellow
ex. 黄身 (きみ) - egg yolk
ex. 黄金 (おうごん) - gold

First girl: なにかしら？このひとたちは？
What the...? Who are all those people over there?
キャーキャー (screaming)
Second girl: みんなおなじ黄いろいシャツをきているわ。They're all wearing the same yellow shirts...
First girl: 黄いろばかりですさまじいわね。
That yellow color is gross.
Second girl: アイドルのおっかけみたいね。
They're probably fans of some pop star.
こっちみてー Look at us!
サインしてー Autograph this!

STEAM

キ

ex. 汽車 (きしゃ) - train
ex. 汽笛 (きてき) - steam whistle
ex. 蒸気船* (じょうきせん) - steamship

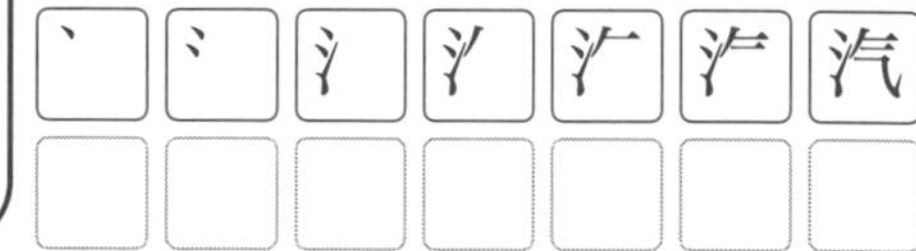

Schoolboy: 汽しゃや汽せんていうのは、じょうきのちからをりようしてうごくのりものなんだよ。
Locomotives and steamboats are powered by steam.

Schoolgirl: そうなんだ。
I see.

GRASS

くさ、ソウ

ex. 草花 (くさばな) - flowering plant
ex. 草木 (くさき) - vegetation
ex. 雑草* (ざっそう) - weed

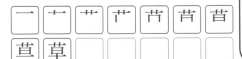

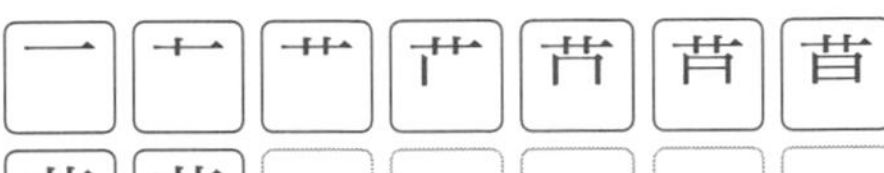

Boy: たった1しゅうかん
しかたっていないのにー!
It has only been a week!

草がこんなに
のびちゃったー!
The weeds have grown so much!

うがーっ!! Aaargh!!

NECK / PRIMARY

くび、シュ

ex. 首 (くび) - neck
ex. 首飾り* (くびかざり) - necklace
ex. 首相* (しゅそう) - prime minister

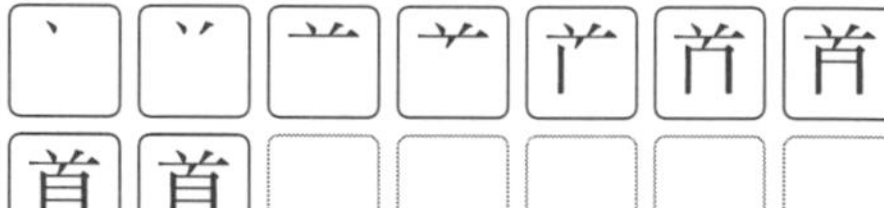

Boy: 首のながいおばけは、ろくろっ首っていうんだって。
The Japanese ghost with the long neck is called a "rokurokubi."

Girl: へぇー…。それって…
I see... Does it have...

Boy: でたー！ A ghost!

ドロドロドロ (sound of ghost appearing)　にょろ〜 (wiggling)

Girl: こんなふうに首がながいのかしら…？くすくすくすくす。
A long neck like this...? Heh heh heh.

GROUP / CLASS

くみ、く(む)、ソ

ex. 組 (くみ) - class; team

ex. 組む (くむ) - to put together

ex. 組織* (そしき) - organization

これから、あか組(ぐみ)としろ組(ぐみ)のつなひきをおこないまーす。
りょうほうの組(くみ)ともじゅんびはいいかな?

Teacher: これから、あか組としろ組の
つなひきをおこないまーす。
We are going to have a tug-of-war
between the red team and the white team.
りょうほうの組ともじゅんびはいいかな？
Are both teams ready?

CLOUD

くも、ウン

ex. 雲 (くも) - cloud
ex. 雨雲 (あまぐも) - rain cloud
ex. 雲海 (うんかい) - sea of clouds

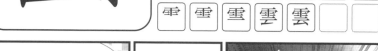

ひこうき雲だね。
これは…
うろこ雲だよ。

Boy on right: ひこうき雲だね。これは…
This is the jet stream.
And these are...

Boy on left: うろこ雲だよ。
Cirrocumulus clouds.

Both boys: (speechless)

ピカッ (flash)
ドーン (bang)
ゴロゴロゴロ (rumble)

Boys (in unison): かみなり雲おおお！
Thunderclouds!

HAIR

け、モウ

ex. 髪の毛* (かみのけ) - hair
ex. 毛虫 (けむし) - caterpillar
ex. 毛筆* (もうひつ) - paintbrush

Girl: だいぶかみの毛ものびたなー。
My hair has gotten pretty long.

PUBLIC

コウ

ex. 公共 (こうきょう) - public
ex. 公平 (こうへい) - fairness
ex. 主人公 (しゅじんこう) - main character

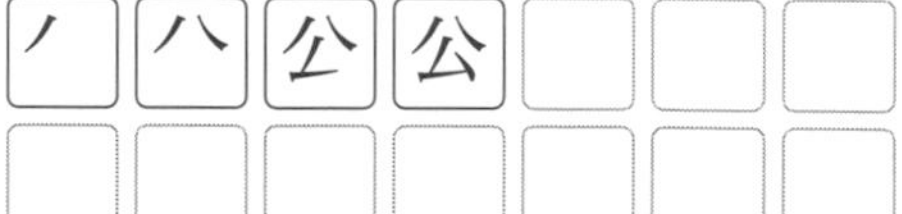

ぶんかさいのげきの
しゅじん公(こう)は
かれにけっていしました!
!?
わー
わあああ
パチ
パチ
パチ
パチ
さんせーい!

こんなかっこで公(こう)
きょうのばしょに
なんかでられないよ〜!
にあってるよー。
こんなの、
公(こう)へいじゃないよ!

Announcement: ぶんかさいのげきのしゅじん公はかれにけっていしました!
We've decided he's going to be the lead in the school play!
わあああ (cheering) パチパチ (clapping)
Students: さんせーい! We agree!
Boy: こんなかっこで公きょうのばしょになんかでられないよ〜!
I can't wear a costume like this in public!
Girl: にあってるよー。But it's so you!
Boy: こんなの、公へいじゃないよ!
This isn't fair!

VOICE

こえ、セイ

ex. 大声 (おおごえ) - large voice
ex. 声優* (せいゆう) - voice actor/actress
ex. 声援* (せいえん) - cheering

First girl: おはよー。きのうのゆうえんちはどうだった？
Good morning. How was the amusement park yesterday?

Second girl: (speechless)

Second girl: ぜっきょうマシンにたくさんのって、おお声でさけんだら…声かれちゃって…。 I rode a lot of roller coasters and screamed so much that my voice became hoarse...

First girl: わっ！すごいガラガラ声！
Wow! What a croaky voice!

FINE / THIN

こま(か)、こま(かい)、ほそ(い)、サイ

ex. 細かい (こまかい) - small; fine; detail
ex. 細い (ほそい) - thin
ex. 細胞* (さいぼう) - cell

じゃあ、よていどおり
あのきかくは
すすめてね。
トントン
わかったわ。
まかせて。

しょう細(さい)は
あのかみに
かいてあるから。
こくっ

びっちり
細(こま)か
すぎるよー…。

First schoolgirl: じゃあ、よていどおりあのきかくはすすめてね。 So, please continue this project as we'd discussed.

トントン (tap tap)

Second schoolgirl: わかったわ。まかせて。Got it! Leave it to me.

First schoolgirl: しょう細はあのかみにかいてあるから。The details are on that page over there.

こくっ (nodding yes)

びっちり (lots of fine print)

Second schoolgirl: 細かすぎるよー。 There are too many fine details.

RICE

こめ、ベイ、マイ

ex. 米 (こめ) - rice

ex. 白米 (はくまい) - white rice

ex. 米国 (べいこく) - United States

Girl: たきたてのお米っていいにおいー！
Freshly cooked rice smells so good!

ほわんほわん (sound of steam rising)

TALENT / AGE

サイ

ex. 才能 (さいのう) - talent
ex. 五才 (ごさい) - 5 years old
ex. 漫才* (まんざい) - comedian

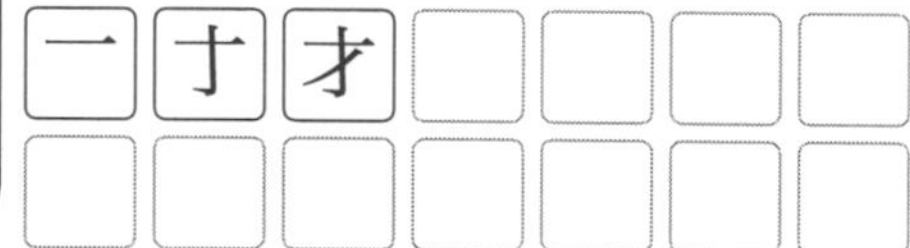

Girl: わたしってなんにも才のうがないなぁ…。
I have no talents at all...

ハァ… (sigh) ぽんっ (pat)

Boy: そんなことないよ!
That's not true!

Boy: きっときみにもすごい才のうがあるよ!
You must have some amazing skill!

Girl: たとえばどんな?
Such as?

Boy: …えっと…。えー…。
Well... Umm...

どよーん (sound of dissapointment)

Girl: (speechless)

FINGER

さ(す)、ゆび、シ

ex. 指輪* (ゆびわ) - ring
ex. 親指 (おやゆび) - thumb
ex. 指示* (しじ) - instruction

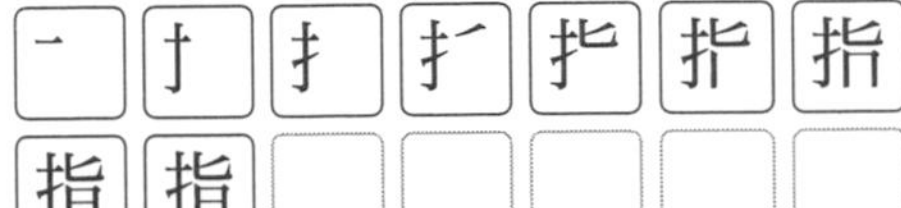

さいきん指もとがさみしいから
指わがほしいなぁ…っておもうの〜。
サッ
ちらっ
!

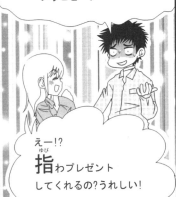

それって…ぼくに
プレゼントしろって
いうこと……?

えー!?
指わプレゼント
してくれるの?うれしい!

Girl: さいきん指もとがさみしいから指わがほしいなぁ…っておもうの〜。 Lately my fingers have been looking so plain, I think I want a ring...

サッ (flick of the hand)

ちらっ (glance)

Boy: それって…ぼくにプレゼントしろっていうこと…? Are you saying I should get you one?

Girl: えー!?指わプレゼントしてくれるの?うれしい! Huh!? You're going to get me a ring? I'm so happy!

COUNTRY HOME

さと、り

ex. 里 (さと) - country home; village
ex. 古里 (ふるさと) - hometown
ex. 里帰り (さとがえり) - visiting one's parents

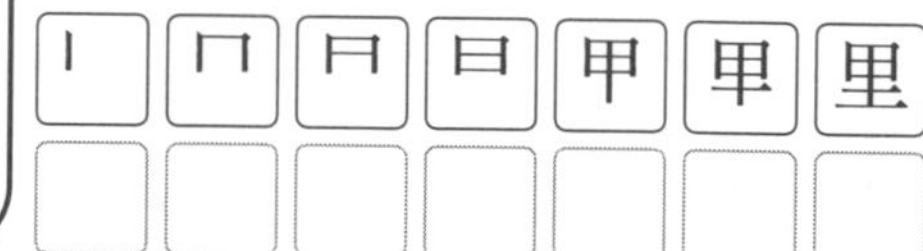

かやぶきやねのおうちが
たくさんあるー!
すごいなぁ。
あっちにはたんぼだ!

ここでは、むかしながらの
里(さと)でのせいかつが
たいけんできるんだよ。
里(さと)でのせいかつを
したことがないから
たのしみ〜。

Girl: かやぶきやねのおうちがたくさんあるー！すごいなぁ。
There are many thatch-roofed houses! It's amazing!
あっちにはたんぼだ！
And the farm is over there!

Boy: ここでは、むかしながらの里でのせいかつがたいけんできるんだよ。
Here you can see how life was in an old-time country home.

Girl: 里でのせいかつをしたことないからたのしみ〜。 I've never experienced village life so I'm looking forward to it.

COUNT

サン

ex. 算数 (さんすう) - arithmetic
ex. 足し算 (たしざん) - addition
ex. 引き算 (ひきざん) - subtraction

Boy: けい算きがなかったころは、
そろばんがけい算きがわりだったんだよなー。
There used to be a time when we would count using an abacus rather than a calculator.
パチパチ (click click)

WRITE DOWN

しる(す)、キ

ex. 記す (しるす) - to write down; to note
ex. 記者 (きしゃ) - journalist; reporter
ex. 記事 (きじ) - newspaper article

記(き)じをかかなくちゃ
しめきりに
なってしまう！
ガリガリ

記(き)しゃのしごとも
らくじゃないな〜……。
パタパタ

Man: 記しゃかいけんが
はじまるぞー！
いそげ〜！
The press conference
is starting soon!
I have to hurry!

だだだだ (dashing)

記じをかかなくちゃ
しめきりになってしまう！
I have to write this article
before the deadline.

ガリガリガリ (pencil on paper)

バッ (sound of paper being tossed)

記しゃのしごとも
らくじゃないな〜…。
It is not easy being
a journalist...

パタパタ (fanning)

LINE

セン

ex. 直線 (ちょくせん) - straight line
ex. 線香* (せんこう) - incense stick
ex. 線路* (せんろ) - track

Son: なにそれ?
What is that?

Mother: はなびよ。
It's a firework.

Mother: 線こうはなびっていうはなびなの。
きれいね。*
This is called a sparkler.
Isn't it pretty?

パチパチ (crackle crackle)

*The word for sparkler (せんこうはなび) combines the kanji for incense stick (線香) and fireworks (花火).

GROW UP

そだ(つ)、そだ(てる)、イク

ex. 育てる (そだてる) - to grow up
ex. 教育 (きょういく) - education
ex. 育児* (いくじ) - child care

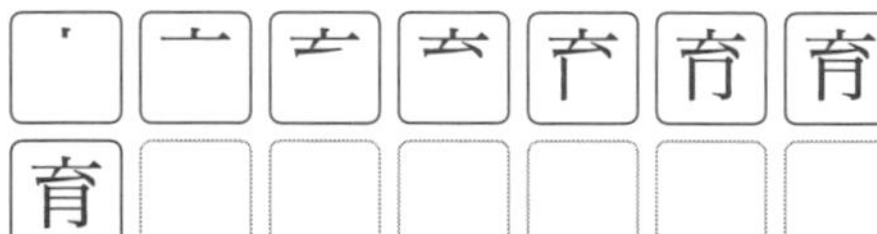

Boy: たしかに…
おおきく育ったらいいなぁ
とはおもったけど…。
Sure I wanted it to grow
to be big, but...

うんうん (nodding)

Girl: わぁぁぁ。
Wow…

Boy: 育ちすぎちゃったみたいだなぁ。
It looks like it got a little too big.

BAMBOO

たけ、チク

ex. 竹林 (ちくりん) - bamboo thicket
ex. 竹垣* (たけがけ) - bamboo fence
ex. 竹の子 (たけのこ) - bamboo shoots

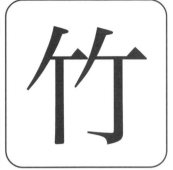

First boy: 竹とりものがたりってむかしばなししってる? Have you ever heard *The Tale of the Bamboo Cutter*?

ギコギコ (cutting noise)

Second boy: しってるよ。Sure.

Second boy: こんなふうにおじいさんが竹をきると、なかからおんなのこがでてくるんでしょ? An old man goes out to cut bamboo like we are, and finds a girl inside, right?

パカッ (pop) *Girl:* こんにちは。Hey there.

Boys (together): ほんとうにいたー！ It's true!

FIX / DIRECT

ただ(ちに)、なお(す)、ジキ、チョク

ex. 直ちに (ただちに) - directly; immediately
ex. 直す (なおす) - to fix
ex. 正直 (しょうじき) - honesty

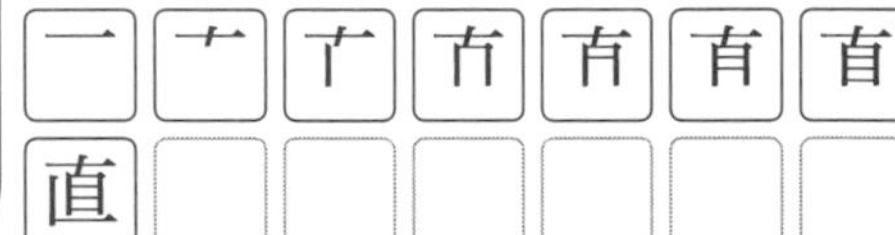

あぁ〜。
じてんしゃがパンク
しちゃった…。
シュ

Boy: ああ〜。
じてんしゃがパンク
しちゃった…。
Oh, man...My bike has a flat tire.

プシュー (pssst...)

Boy: がっこうのかえりにじてんしゃやさんで
直してもらわないと。
I'll have to get it fixed at the bike shop on my way home from school.

VALLEY

たに、コク

ex. 谷 (たに) - valley
ex. 谷川 (たにがわ) - mountain stream
ex. 谷間 (たにま) - ravine

First boy: この谷、すごくふかいね〜。
This is such a deep valley.
すごいけい谷〜！
What an amazing valley!

ヒュオオオオ (howling wind)

Second boy: (speechless)

Second boy: こしがぬけちゃって、うごけないよー…。
I'm so scared of heights I can't move...

First boy: (speechless)

BALL

たま、ギョク

ex. 目玉 (めだま) - eyeball
ex. 水玉 (みずたま) - polkadot
ex. お手玉 (おてだま) - juggling

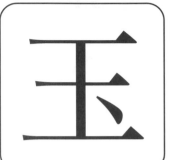

Boy: 玉のり！
I'm balancing on this ball!
ド… (sound of boy balancing on the ball)

おて玉！ I can juggle!
ポンポン (sound of throwing the balls)
いてっ！ Ouch!
ポコポコ (sound of balls hitting boy's head)

TEMPLE

てら、ジ

ex. お寺 (おてら) - temple

ex. 山寺 (やまでら) - mountain temple

ex. 寺男 (てらおとこ) - (male) temple worker

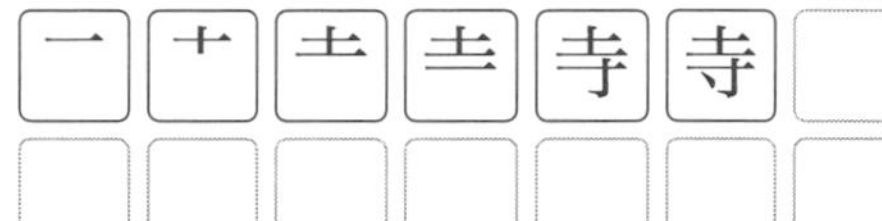

みて。
ずいぶんふるそうな
お寺(てら)があるよ。
おもむきがある
お寺(てら)だね。

First girl: みて。ずいぶんふるそうなお寺があるよ。
Look. There's a really old temple.

Second girl: おもむきがあるお寺だね。
This temple sure has a certain elegance about it.

POINTS / SCORE

テン

ex. 点検* (てんけん) - inspection
ex. 点滅* (てんめつ) - flashing
ex. 減点* (げんてん) - subtract

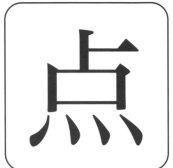

あれ?
エンジンのちょうしが
わるいのかなぁ…?
ガガガガが

ひごろからの
点けんをこころがけないとね。
さいきん
さぼっていたからなー。
ふい〜…

Man: あれ？エンジンのちょうしがわるいのかなぁ…？
Hmm? I wonder if something's wrong with the engine...

ガガガガ (rattling)

ふい〜 (phew)

ひごろからの点けんをこころがけないとね。
I must remember to do regular inspections.

さいきんさぼっていたかれあなー。
I haven't been taking good care of my car lately...

DOOR

と、コ

ex. 戸 (と) - door
ex. 江戸 (えど) - old name of Tokyo
ex. 戸籍* (こせき) - census

Girl: いえの戸にぜんぶかぎをかけているの？
Are you locking all the doors in the house?

えっへん (Ahem!)

Boy: 戸じまりはたいせつだからね。
Security is important.

Boy: おかげで戸のかぎが、こんなにたくさんになっちゃった…。
That's why I have so many keys...

Girl: うわっ。
Whoa!

じゃらっ (jingling)

FAR / DISTANT

とお(い)、エン

ex. 遠い (とおい) - far; distant
ex. 遠足 (えんそく) - trip
ex. 遠近法* (えんきんほう) - perspective

一	十	土	士	吉	吉	声
袁	袁	袁	遠	遠	遠	

Boy: あの遠くにみえるのがふじさんだな。
That one in the distance must be Mt. Fuji.

ANIMAL-LIKE SOUND

な(く)、な(らす)、な(る)、メイ

ex. 鳴き声 (なきごえ) - cry; roar
ex. 悲鳴* (ひめい) - shriek; scream
ex. 雷鳴* (らいめい) - thunder

きみのうちのネコが鳴いているみたいだけどどうしたのかな?
あぁ、それはねかんたんよ。

にゃーーん
ごはんのじかんがまちきれなくて鳴いているのよ。

First girl: きみのうちのネコが鳴いているみたいだけどどうしたのかな?
It seems like your cat is crying. Do you think he's OK?

Second girl: あぁ、それはねかんたんよ。Oh, that's nothing.

Cat: にゃーん
Meow!

Second girl: ごはんのじかんがまちきれなくて鳴いているのよ。
He's meowing because he can't wait for dinner.

TOOTH

は、シ

ex. 虫歯 (むしば) - cavity
ex. 歯磨き* (はみがき) - toothpaste
ex. 歯科医 (しかい) - dentist

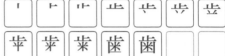

Mother: 歯みがきしなさいね。
Make sure you brush your teeth.
Son: めんどうだからいや!
I don't want to! It's too much work!
Mother: 歯みがきしないとむし歯になってたいへんよ〜!
If you don't brush your teeth, you'll get cavities and you'll hate it!
ギロ (staring)　ドロドロドロ (sound of something threatening)

シャカシャカシャカ
(brush brush)
Mother: ふふふ。
Heh heh...

FEATHER

は、はね

ex. 羽 (はね) - feather; plume; wing
ex. 羽根突き* (はねつき) - shuttlecock
ex. 羽音 (はおと) - buzz; hum

Girl: まるで羽がはえて
とんでいるみたい〜。
I feel like I could sprout
wings and fly away...

フワ…フワ… (sound of flying away)
どうしてかしら?
I wonder why that is?

あら…!?ほんとうにとんでいるわ!
What!? I'm really flying!
羽がはえたんだわ!
I must have grown wings!

バサバサ (flap flap)

Boy: はやくきづいてくれー!
Wake up and smell the coffee!

NOSE

はな

ex. 鼻水 (はなみず) - runny nose
ex. 鼻声 (はなごえ) - nasal voice
ex. 鼻炎* (びえん) - nasal inflammation

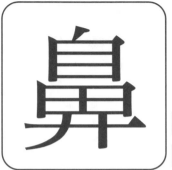

ちーん
(sound made when blowing the nose)

Sister: かぜ?かふんしょう?
Do you have a cold? Or hay fever?

Brother: どっちかなぁ…。
I'm not sure which...

Brother: 鼻かみすぎでいたいよー。
I blew my nose so much it hurts.

ヒリヒリ (stinging pain)

Sister: 鼻がまっかだよ!
Your nose is all red!

WOODS

はやし、リン

ex. 林 (はやし) - woods
ex. 林道 (りんどう) - hiking path
ex. 林業 (りんぎょう) - forestry

First boy scout: キャンプじょうにはこの林をとおるんだね。
We have to hike through these woods to get to the campsite.

Second boy scout: 林のむこうがキャンプじょうなんだね。たのしみだな。
So it's just beyond these woods. I sure am excited!

Sign: キャンプじょう (Campground)

CAUSE / FIELD

はら、ゲン

ex. 原っぱ (はらっぱ) - open field
ex. 原因* (げんいん) - cause
ex. 原稿* (げんこう) - manuscript

ぐあいがわるそうね。
だいじょうぶ?
うー…ん。

原いんは、
きのうみずあびをした
せいだと思う…。
あんなにさむい
なかみずあそび
したの!?

Sister: ぐあいがわるそうね。だいじょうぶ？ You don't look so good. Are you all right?
Brother: うーん。 Not really...
Brother: 原いんは、きのうみずあびをしたせいだと思う…。I think it's 'cause I went swimming in the river...
Sister: あんなにさむいなかみずあそびしたの！？ You were playing in the water during this cold weather!?

CLEAR WEATHER

は(らす)、は(れる)、セイ

ex. 晴れ (はれ) - clear weather
ex. 快晴* (かいせい) - good weather
ex. 晴れ着 (はれぎ) - one's best clothes

さっきまであめだったのにすっかり晴(は)れたみたい。
晴(は)れてよかったー。

College student: さっきまであめだったのにすっかり晴れたみたい。
It was raining a while ago but it seems to have cleared up.
晴れてよかったー。
I'm so glad the sun came out.

ORDER / ONE'S TURN

バン

ex. 番号* (ばんごう) - number
ex. 順番* (じゅんばん) - order
ex. 番犬 (ばんけん) - watchdog

First student: なん番めだった？ ぼくは6番め。
When is your turn?
I'm sixth.

Second student: 10番めだったよ。
I'm number ten.

Teacher's aid: 番ごうじゅんにうけつけしますのでじゅん番にならんでください。
We will proceed in order, so please line up.

Sign: うけつけ (Reception)

LIGHT

ひかり、ひか(る)、コウ

ex. 光る (ひかる) - to shine
ex. 観光* (かんこう) - sightseeing
ex. 日光 (にっこう) - sunlight

ピッカー (flash)

Girl: まぶしい！なにかしら、あの光！？
Too bright!
What is that light!?

ピカピカピカ (twinkle twinkle)

おじいちゃんのあたまが光っていたの〜！？
Grandpa's shiny head!?

PULL

ひ(く)、ひ(ける)、イン

ex. 引金 (ひきがね) - trigger
ex. 引力 (いんりょく) - gravity
ex. 吸引* (きゅういん) - absorption

Boy: このドアいくら引いても
あかない〜！
I keep pulling on this door
but it won't open!

Girl: え！？
Huh!?

Boy: あ…。Oh...
引くんじゃなくて
おすんだった…。
I'm supposed to push, not pull.

カチャ (click)

Girl: (speechless)

FAT / THICK

ふと(い)、ふと(る)、タ、タイ

ex. 太る (ふとる) - to become fat
ex. 丸太 (まるた) - log
ex. 太平洋 (たいへいよう) - Pacific Ocean

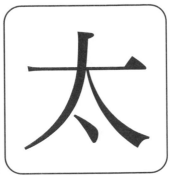

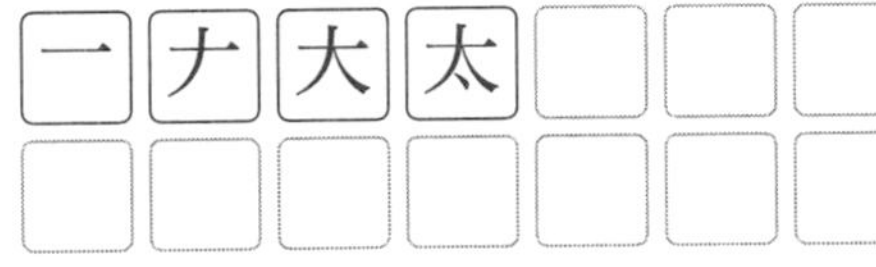
一
ナ
大
太

えええええ!? も…もしかして
さとうくんなの!?
ガーん…
でっぷり
サッカーやめたら
すごい太っちゃって。

Girl: えええええ！？も…もしかしてさとうくんなの！？
Whaaat!? Is... is that really you, Sato!?

ガーン… (shocked)

でっぷり (sound of lots of weight)

Sato: サッカーやめたらすごい太っちゃって。
I've kinda become fat since I stopped playing soccer.

船

BOAT / VESSEL

ふな、ふね、セン

ex. 船 (ふね) - ship
ex. 船出 (ふなで) - setting sail
ex. 船酔い* (ふなよい) - seasickness

ごうかきゃく船でのたびって、すてきよねー。してみたいわぁ。
そうね。
うっとり…

ああっ。でも、船よいってあるのかしら!?だったらたいへんね。
はっ
だいじょうぶだとおもうけど。

First girl: ごうかきゃく船でのたびって、すてきよねー。してみたいわぁ。
A cruise sounds wonderful.
I'd love to go on one.

Second girl: そうね。Yeah.

うっとり… (sound of fascination)

First girl: ああっ。でも、船よいってあるのかしら！？だったらたいへんね。Oh, but, what if I got seasick!? That would stink!

はっ (gasp)

Second girl: だいじょうぶだとおもうけど。I think you'd be fine...

STAR

ほし、セイ

ex. 流れ星 (ながれぼし) - shooting star
ex. 星占い (ほしうらない) - horoscope
ex. 火星 (かせい) - Mars

すってーん
(tripping sound)
First boy: だいじょうぶか!?
Are you all right!?

Second boy: あれれれ?お星さまがたくさんみえる〜。星がきれいだなぁ〜。
Huh? I can see lots of stars.
Stars sure are purdy...
くわんくわん (dizzy)
First boy: (speechless)

INTERSECTION

ま(ざる)、まじ(える)、まじ(わる)、コウ

ex. 交わる (まじわる) - to cross
ex. 交差点 (こうさてん) - crosswalk
ex. 交番* (こうばん) - police box

そうね、交(こう)さてんだけじゃなく交(こう)つうルールはまもろうね。
ぼく、がんばって交(こう)つうルールをきちんとまもるよ。

Son: ぼく、がんばって交つうルールをきちんとまもるよ。
I'll do my best to follow the rules when crossing.

Mother: そうね、交さてんだけじゃなく交ルールはまもろうね。
That's right, and we should follow the rules everywhere, not just at crosswalks.

CIRCLE / ROUND

まる、まる(い)、まる(める)、ガン

ex. 丸い (まるい) - round
ex. 日の丸 (ひのまる) - the Japanese flag
ex. 弾丸* (だんがん) - bullet

First boy: なんで、へやに
丸いきんぞくの
かたまりがあるの？
Why is there a round lump of metal in your room?

Second boy: あれ？ Oh, that?

Second boy: ほう丸なげをしているんだ。
いえでもれんしゅうするから。
'Cause I throw shot put, and I like to practice at home.

ひょい (picking something up casually)

First boy: そうだったんだ。Gotcha.

TURN / SPIN

まわ(す)、まわ(る)、カイ

ex. 回る (まわる) - to turn
ex. 次回 (じかい) - next time
ex. 回数* (かいすう) - number of times

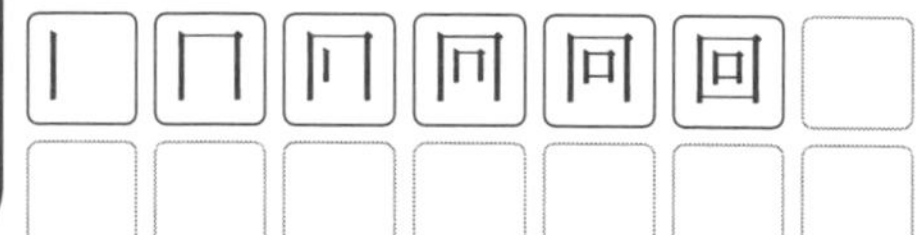

Teacher: みんな、コマは
よく回ったかな?
Did everyone's tops
spin well?
それでは、こん回の
じっけんはここまで。
That's it for today's lab.

Student: じ回はいつですか?
When's our next lab?

Teacher: じ回のじっけんは、らいしゅう
することにします。
We'll have another lab next week.

Students (in unison): はーい
Yes, sir!

BODY

身

み、シン

ex. 身体 (しんたい) - body; health
ex. 身長 (しんちょう) - height
ex. 中身 (なかみ) - contents; substance

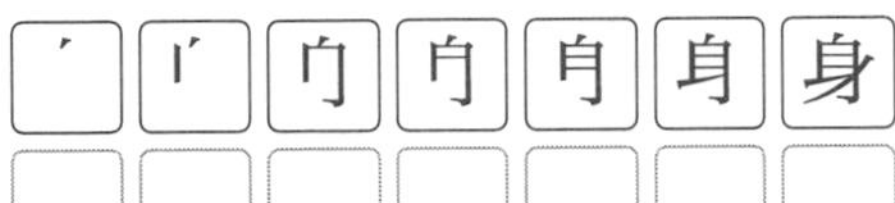

身(しん)たいそくていの
けっかどうだった?

きょねんより身(しん)ちょうが
5センチのびていたよ。
わたしはあまり
身(しん)ちょうのびて
いなかった…。

Girl: 身たいそくていの
けっかどうだった？
How did your health exam turn out?

Boy: きょねんより身ちょうが5センチ
のびていたよ。
I've grown 5 centimeters since last year.

Girl: わたしはあまり身ちょう
のびていなかった。
I haven't really gotten any taller...

EAR

みみ

ex. 耳栓* (みみせん) - earplug
ex. 耳輪* (みみわ) - earring
ex. 耳垢* (みみあか) - earwax

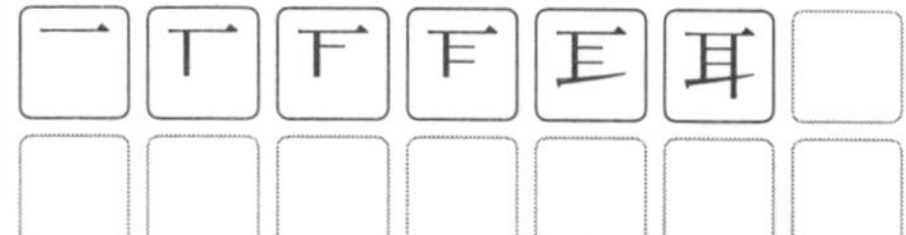

しゅくだいは
すませたの?
へやは
かたづけた?
ぎくっ
まんが4

Mother: しゅくだいはすませたの？
Did you finish your homework?
へやはかたづけた？
Did you clean up your room?

ぎくっ (jumpy)

Son: それ、耳にたこができるほどきいたよ〜。
I've heard that so many times...
耳がいたいくらいだよ…。
My ears are beginning to hurt...

Mother: だったらさっさとすませなさい！
Then do it now!

ペキペキ (sound of cracking knuckles)

WHEAT

むぎ

ex. 麦畑 (むぎばたけ) - wheat field
ex. 小麦粉* (こむぎこ) - wheat flour
ex. 麦わら帽子 (むぎわらぼうし) - straw hat

First girl: その麦わらぼうしよくにあっているわよ。
That straw hat looks good on you.

Second girl: ありがとう！
Thank you!

INSECT

むし、チュウ

ex. 虫除け* (むしよけ) - insect repellent
ex. 虫眼鏡 (むしめがね) - magnifying glass
ex. 虫酸* (むしず) - heartburn

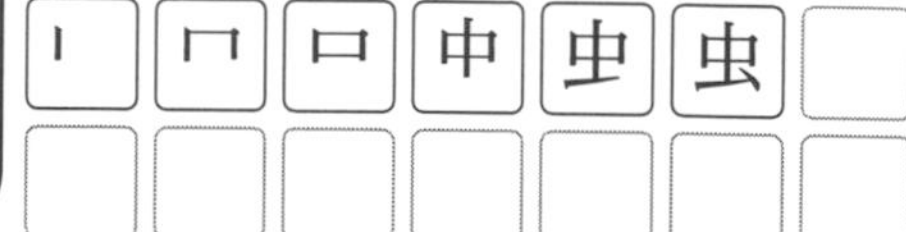

わたし虫がすごくにがてなの…。
け虫でしょ…。
ゴキブリでしょ。
わたしもにがて…。
うん。
うん。

……? どうしたの?
……。

カク…
カク…
きっと虫のことをかんがえてきぜつしたのよ。

First girl: わたし虫がすごくにがてなの…。
I can't stand insects...
け虫でしょ…。ゴキブリでしょ。
Caterpillars... Cockroaches...

Second girl: わたしもにがて…。
I can't stand them either...

Third girl: うん。うん。Totally.

Second girl: …? どうしたの?
Huh? What's wrong?

カクカク (bones rattling)

Third girl: きっと虫のことをかんがえてきぜつしたのよ。
She must've freaked out from thinking about bugs so much.

VILLAGE

むら、ソン

ex. 村人 (むらびと) - villager
ex. 漁村 (ぎょそん) - fishing village
ex. 農村 (のうそん) - farm village

Boy: こんなやまおくに村なんて
あるのかなぁ…。
I wonder if there's really
a village this deep in the woods.

ガサガサ (rustling)

村だ！村びともいるぞ。
A village! And there are
villagers too!

FOREST

もり、シン

ex. 森 (もり) - forest
ex. 森林 (しんりん) - the woods
ex. 森林火災* (しんりんかさい) - forest fire

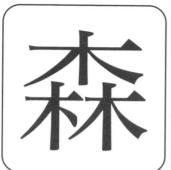

Girl: こういうちいさなきが、たくさんおおきくなって森になるんだね。
A bunch of little trees just like this one will someday become a forest.

ARROW

や

ex. 矢先 (やさき) - arrowhead
ex. 矢柄* (やがら) - shaft of an arrow
ex. 矢筒* (やづつ) - quiver

Girl: なにをつくっているの？
What are you making?

Boy: 矢さきだよ。いしで
つくっているんだ。
It's an arrowhead. I'm making it out of stone.

Boy: むかしはぼうのさきに矢さきをつけて、かりをしていたんだよ。In the Stone Age, people would attach an arrowhead to the end of a stick for hunting.

Girl: むかしのさいげんをしているのね。
Looks like you're trying to relive the olden days.

SNOW

ゆき、セツ

ex. 雪だるま (ゆきだるま) - snowman
ex. 雪国 (ゆきぐに) - snow country
ex. 風雪 (ふうせつ) - snowstorm

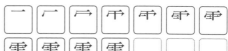

Dogs: わんわん
Woof! Woof!

Boy: 雪がつもってあんなに
よろこんでる。かわいいなぁ。
The dogs are so happy the snow has piled up. How cute!

雪がつもってよろこんだのは
ちいさいころまでだったなぁ…。
Snow piles always made me happy when I was a kid...

ぬくぬく (snuggle)

BOW

ゆみ、キュウ

ex. 弓矢 (ゆみや) - bow and arrow
ex. 弓道 (きゅうどう) - Japanese archery
ex. 弓師* (ゆみし) - bow maker

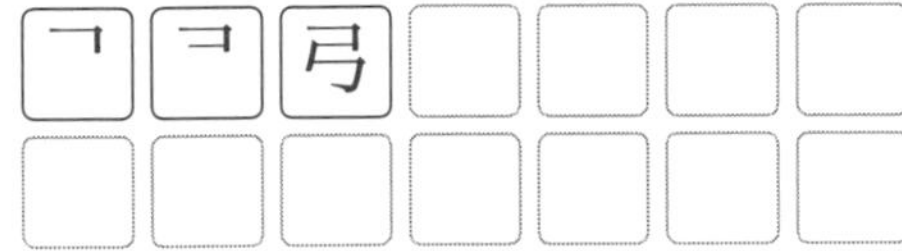

Boy: いったいなんの
おとだろう?
What in the world
is that sound?

パシュッ (whoosh)

タン(thud)

Boy: 弓どうじょうで弓どうの
れんしゅうをしていたんだ。
Someone is practicing
Japanese archery at the dojo.

BAD

わる(い)、アク

ex. 悪い (わるい) - bad

ex. 悪人 (あくにん) - bad guy

ex. 邪悪* (じゃあく) - evil

かわいそうに。
すてられちゃったの?
じつは
悪(あく)にんではなくて
いいひとかも…。
ホッ

Man: ちっ。(clicking of tongue)

Boy: わあ…っ　悪そうな人だ…。こわいなぁ。
Wow... That's one scary-looking dude...Yikes.

にゃー にゃー (cat's meow)

ギロッ (look of anger)

Man: かわいそうに。すてられちゃったの?
Poor baby. Have you been abandoned?

Boy: じつは悪にんではなくて いいひとかも…。Actually, he may not be such a bad guy after all...
ホッ Whew!

WEAK

よわ(い)、よわ(める)、よわ(る)、ジャク

ex. 弱い (よわい) - weak

ex. 弱虫 (よわむし) - coward

ex. 強弱 (きょうじゃく) - strength

弱

ううう〜……。
さむい……。
ガチガチ
ガチガチ
ブルッ

さむいよー!
れいぼうをもっと弱くしてくれよー!
かぜひいちゃうよ。
ごめん、ごめん。
あつがりなんで。

First boy: ううう〜…。さむい…。
Brrr… I'm freezing…

ガチガチ (teeth chattering)

ブルッ (shaking from cold)

First boy: さむいよー! れいぼうをもっと弱くしてくれよー! かぜひいちゃうよ。
It's freezing! Could you turn down the air conditioning? I'm gonna catch a cold!

Second boy: ごめん、ごめん。あつがりなんで。
Sorry, sorry. I'm very sensitive to heat.

REASON

り

ex. 理科 (りか) - science
ex. 理由* (りゆう) - reason
ex. 真理 (しんり) - truth

Boy: しんろきぼうを、ぶんけいにするか
それとも理けいにするか…。
Should I go into humanities?
Or science...
どちらにするか、まよっちゃうなー。
I wonder which one I should pick.

ふむふむ (nodding head)

理かがすきだから
理けいもいいなぁ。
I like my science classes so
science sounds good.
理ゆうとしては
理にかなっているよな。
That should be reason enough.

FEE / MATERIALS

リョウ

ex. 材料* (ざいりょう) - ingredient
ex. 料金 (りょうきん) - fare; fee
ex. 料理 (りょうり) - cooking

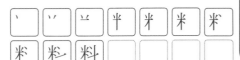

Mother: よーし。料りをはじめるぞー。
All right. Let's start cooking.

Daughter: おかあさん、わたしもてつだう。
Mommy, I'll help.

Mother: じゃあ、そこにあるざい料をあらってくれるかな。
Well then, could you wash the vegetables over there?

Daughter: はーい。
OK.

SEPARATE / ANOTHER

わか(れる)、ベツ

ex. 区別* (くべつ) - distinction
ex. 差別* (さべつ) - discrimination
ex. 別々* (べつべつ) - separately

プレゼントなので、ぬいぐるみを
別べつにつつんでください。

Customer: プレゼントなので、ぬいぐるみを
別べつにつつんでください。
These are gifts, so please wrap each of the stuffed toys separately.

OCEAN / WESTERN

ヨウ

ex. 大西洋 (たいせいよう) - Alantic Ocean

ex. 西洋 (せいよう) - the west; western

ex. 洋服 (ようふく) - Western-style clothes

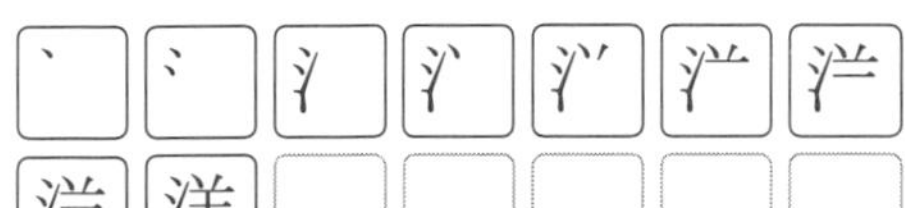

Girl: わぁぁぁぁぁぁぁぁん！！

Waaahhh!!

あしたのデートできる洋ふくどうしよう～。

What clothes should I wear for tomorrow's date?

洋ふくがきまらないよ～。

I don't know what clothes to wear.

TAKE THE TEST!

The Japanese Language Proficiency Test has been held annually throughout the world since 1984. Administered by the Japanese government and the nonprofit Japan Foundation, the test evaluates and certifies the proficiency of non-native speakers of Japanese. There are four levels to the examination: Level 4 for beginners, Level 3 for intermediate students, Level 2 for those who are functionally literate in Japanese, and Level 1 for experts.

This book features 80 of the kanji students will need to know to pass Level 3 of the JLPT. Subsequent volumes in Manga University's *Kanji de Manga* series will help students prepare for the higher levels.

For more information about the Japanese Language Proficiency Test, including examination locations in your country, please visit the Japan Foundation's "JLPT Communications Square" website at http://momo.jpf.go.jp/jlpt/e/about_e.html.

PRACTICE SECTION

KANJI INDEX

The 80 kanji featured in this volume of *Kanji de Manga* are indexed here based on their *on-yomi* and *kun-yomi* readings. This makes it easy to look up any kanji for which you know a pronunciation but cannot remember how the character is written. Because most kanji have more than one reading, you will find those characters listed multiple times in this index.

REAL オタク CAN READ 日本語

(*Translation:* Real Otaku Can Read Japanese)

ISBN 4-921205-02-7

ISBN 4-921205-03-5

ISBN 4-921205-04-3

"A Brilliant Idea! Makes Learning Kanji Fun And Easy!"

–Ronald A. Morse, Professor of Japan Studies, University of Nevada, Las Vegas

Kana de Manga and *Kanji de Manga,* an exciting new series from MANGA UNIVERSITY, uses original manga artwork to teach "otaku" of all ages how to read and write Japanese. With these handy manga-size books at your side, you'll learn the language in no time at all!

www.MANGAUNIVERSITY.com

GLENN KARDY is the editor of several volumes in the renowned *How to Draw Manga* series of art-instruction guides, including *Getting Started*, the first book of its kind to be used at major universities in both the United States (UCLA) and Japan (Waseda). Glenn lives in the Tokyo suburb of Kawaguchi City with his wife, their daughter and a collection of Oakland A's bobblehead dolls.

CHIHIRO HATTORI, niece of legendary manga artist Eiichi Fukui, was a graphics designer at Tokyo-based TechnoArt before turning her attention full-time to her manga career. Chihiro and her husband live in Yokohama, where they enjoy fine food, fast cars and high fashion.

Cover illustrations by Chihiro Hattori
Introduction by Edward Mazza
Art coordinator: Mari Oyama
Translators: RyoRca and Dale Rubin
Production assistant: Shinobu Sendai
Editorial assistant: Peter Johnson